Celebrating A Christ-Centered Christmas

IDEAS FROM A TO Z

Sharon Jaynes

MOODY PRESS
CHICAGO

Design: Ragont Design

Photography: Tim Olive, except for pages 73-74: Jim Whitmer; 87, 88 and 90: Photodisc; 109-110: Wonderfile.

ISBN: 0-8024-1699-3

3 5 7 9 10 8 6 4 2

Printed in the United States of America

To my husband, Steve, and my son, Steven.
Sharing Christmases with you has brought much
joy to my world.

Table of Contents

Acknowledgments

Special thanks to:

My special "tea party" friends, Linda Butler, Miriam Londry, Cissy Smith, and Lysa TerKeurst.

My other two little TerKeurst ladies, Hope in the treasure hunt photo, and Ashley in the crafts for kids photo.

Our visiting college student, Matthew Means, and my little gentleman in Love, 1 Corinthians 13-style, Joshua Swope, and my princess in the Jesse Tree, Victoria Long.

Tim Olive, a master of photography who captures the beauty of light and reflects the light of Christ in his work.

Dave DeWit and Greg Thornton of Moody Press, who made working with Tim possible.

Sue Maizy for her penmanship, Mary Ruth Diffy for her scavenger hunting, and Mary Kay McCrachen for sharing her candy cane tradition.

Two special ladies who allowed me to include their ideas for the soft-sculpted nativity set, Jo Ellen Burns and Marcia Gallerini.

Bethany Martin for her calligraphy talent in creating the "Hark! the Herald Angels Sing" scroll.

And Janet Kobobel Grant, my agent, editor, and friend.

Celebrating A Christ-Centered Christmas

Once a little girl named Mary Beth found herself caught in the pre-Christmas swirl of activity. Her dad was scurrying about, loaded down with bundles and burdens. Her mom, under the pressure of preparing for the great occasion, had succumbed to tears several times. The little girl tried to help her weary parents but found she was often in the way.

"Not now, Mary Beth. Can't you see I'm busy?" each parent would say.

Finally, near tears herself, Mary Beth was hustled off to bed. There, as she knelt to pray the Lord's Prayer, her heart and tongue became intertwined. "Forgive us our Christmases as we forgive those who Christmas against us," she said.[1]

Perhaps Mary Beth's prayer wasn't so far from the truth. Many times we leave Christ out of Christmas. Many times our Christmas spirit is not of good will but of exhaustion, causing us to trample on our loved ones' feelings. And many times we're so busy planning the birthday celebration that we forget to invite the guest of honor.

Imagine for a moment that you never have heard the Christmas story, and you visit a shopping mall on December 22. You listen to the music being played over the intercom system and eavesdrop on a few shoppers' conversations. Next, you stop by a greeting card shop and browse through the rows of red and green envelopes with cards sporting colorful and comical messages. Window displays grab your attention, enticing last-minute shoppers with promises of low prices. Stress-laden people rush by carrying stacks of boxes in various shapes and sizes. What conclusions would you draw about the event that culminates on December 25?

Much has changed since the God of the universe decorated the night sky with the star of Bethlehem and directed the choir of angels in a chorus announcing our Savior's birth. But the commercialism doesn't have to rule in our hearts and homes. This year, let's focus on the Christ child.

As we turn our eyes to the Babe in the manger, Christmas is transformed from a dreaded obligation and a major retail event. It becomes a time of joyous celebration, honoring the One who came to give us eternal life and worshipping our heavenly Father.

Join me now as we explore together, A - Z, ways to celebrate a Christ-centered Christmas.

Advent, a Time to Prepare

Anticipating a big event stirs the senses and builds excitement. Ask any mother-to-be surrounded by gifts at a baby shower or a betrothed couple at an engagement party. They will tell you that the months and weeks leading up to the big event are some of the most joyous days of life.

So it is with advent. The word *advent* refers to the coming or arrival of Jesus Christ and traditionally consists of the four Sundays prior to Christmas Day. Advent is a time for us to focus on the Scriptures that herald Jesus' birth and to prepare our hearts to celebrate anew His coming.

A traditional part of advent that you might want to incorporate into your celebration is a wreath consisting of four candles evenly spaced around its circumference with one candle in the center. The circle represents God's eternal love that knows no end, and the wreath's greenery represents the everlasting life that Christ brings. Each candle symbolizes an important aspect of Christ's birth and is lit on a particular Sunday in advent.

The first candle is lit on the first Sunday of advent, shortly after November 30. It is called the prophecy candle and reminds us that Jesus' coming was prophesied hundreds of years before He was born. The candle's purple color represents Christ's royalty and His title, the King of Kings.

Suggested Bible reading: Isaiah 9:2-6, Luke 1:30-35.

The second candle, lit on the second Sunday of advent along with the first candle, is the Bethlehem candle, reminding us where Jesus was born. It too is purple, for our King who was born in the manger.

Suggested Bible reading: Micah 5:2, Luke 2:1-7.

The third candle, lit on the third Sunday of advent along with the first two candles, is the shepherds' candle. We are reminded that God sent the angels to proclaim His arrival to common man and that He uses common folks still today to spread the good news of Christ. This candle is pink or rose and represents God's love and faithfulness.

Suggested Bible reading: Isaiah 52:7, Luke 2:8-12.

The fourth candle, lit on the fourth Sunday of advent, is the angels' candle. When we light this flame, we are reminded of the heavenly hosts who proclaimed Christ's arrival with, "Behold, I bring you good news of a great joy!" The angel candle is also purple, reminding us that the angels proclaimed a king's birth.

As the number of lighted candles increases, the room becomes brighter, reminding us that the time for the Light of the World to arrive is drawing near.

Suggested Bible reading: Ezekiel 34:23, Luke 2:13-20.

The fifth candle, the Christ candle, rests in the center of the wreath and is lit on Christmas Eve. This candle is white, symbolizing Christ's holiness, purity, and perfection. In our home, we use a large white candle that burns the entire Christmas Day.

Suggested Bible reading: Isaiah 9:2-6, John 1:6-13.

The advent wreath can be elaborate, made with fresh holly, spruce, or magnolia and intertwined with lush velvet ribbon and glass ornaments added for decoration. Or it can be as simple as an inverted aluminum pie pan with small X's cut where the candles are inserted.

B Birthday Party for Jesus

At what age do we tire of birthday parties? Twelve? Twenty? Sixty? Ninety? The truth is, almost everyone cherishes the idea of having his or her life celebrated by loved ones. Perhaps that's why "Happy Birthday to You" is the most widely sung tune around the globe.

What better way to celebrate a Christ-centered Christmas than by hosting a birthday party for Jesus? Chances are many children in your neighborhood are unclear about Christmas's true meaning. All children enjoy birthday parties and would love to join the celebration. Here are a few ideas to get you started:

❖ Create a party invitation that exudes excitement, activity, and fun.

❖ Ask each child to bring an inexpensive, gender-neutral gift to exchange.

❖ Decorate the room as you would for any other birthday party: streamers, balloons, confetti, and a birthday banner.

❖ During the party, play games with a Christmas twist: musical chairs with Christmas music, bingo using the word "angel" instead of "bingo," pin the tail on the donkey. (Show a picture of Mary riding to Bethlehem on a donkey.)

❖ Have each child make a simple Christmas craft as a take-home gift, such as the ones mentioned under the letter "Q" of this book.

❖ Number the gifts that the children bring and write the number of each on a slip of paper. Then have each child pick a number to determine which gift he or she gets to keep. Explain that Jesus was the first Christmas gift. God gave His Son as a gift to take away our sins. When we accept Him as our Savior, He comes to live in our hearts, and we live forever in heaven with Him. Now, at Christmastime, we give gifts to each other to remind us of God's great gift to us.

❖ Of course, no birthday party is complete without a cake. Decorate the cake with candles and sing "Happy Birthday" to Jesus.

❖ Read the Christmas story from Luke 2 and have the children act it out. Prepare ahead of time some simple costumes: sheets and rope belts for shepherds, Mary, and Joseph; halos and wings for angels; beautifully wrapped gift boxes and bathrobes for the wise men; a baby doll as Jesus; a pillow for the hump in the camel's back; a fuzzy white blanket for the sheep. When the parents come to pick up their children, invite them in to see the performance. Not only will you minister to the children, but you will also touch their parents' hearts.

Happy birthday, Jesus!

Customized Candy Canes

*P*erhaps one of the sweetest Christmas traditions is giving and receiving candy canes. Many who enjoy eating this treat or hanging the canes on their trees are unaware of the symbolism that is rooted in the person of Jesus Christ.

By my door I keep a basket of candy canes with the following note attached to each cane, ready to hand to all my guests.

The familiar candy cane is such an old Christmas symbol, many of us have forgotten its meaning. The shape, like a shepherd's staff, symbolizes the guidance and protection of our Good Shepherd. Upside down, the cane forms the letter "J" for Jesus. The color red symbolizes the atoning sacrifice of Christ's shed blood. White symbolizes the Savior's purity and holiness. The smaller, thinner stripes represent the sacrifices one makes as a Christian. The candy cane's fragrance is much like that of hyssop, an herb used during Bible times for therapeutic purposes. This represents the healing power of Jesus. Scripture says, "By His stripes we are healed." The candy cane is sweet and meant to be broken and shared, just as His body was broken for us that we might share in His inheritance. Merry Christmas!

To begin this holiday tradition in your home, type the above message to fit in a 4″ x 4″ square (four of the paragraphs will fit on one page). Photocopy

the message onto green paper. Cut out each square and fold the square paper

in half and then in half again,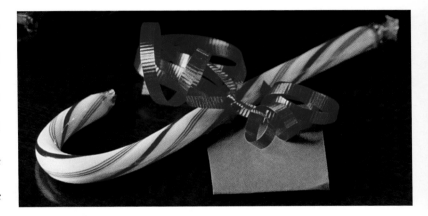

keeping it in the shape of a

square. Punch a hole in a corner,

being careful no words appear in

that area, and fasten the message

to the neck of the candy cane

with ample amounts of red curling ribbon. Place a basket of the candy canes

by your door and give to all who enter your joyful home. You also might

want to hand them out to the grocery store cashier, the bank teller, the mail

carrier, and anyone else you feel needs a bit of holiday cheer.

Dinner Conversation

After a day of Moms running errands and sitting in carpool lines, Dads staring at a computer screen and

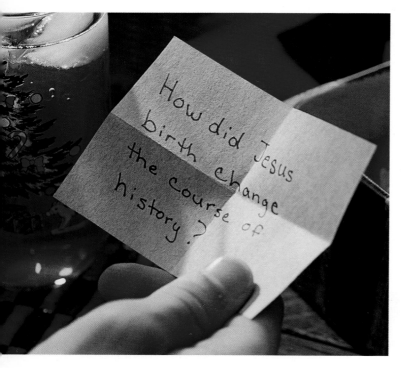

How did Jesus birth change the course of history?

making sales calls, not to mention . Junior's rushing from a packed school schedule to basketball practice, it's a relief to finally sit down as a family and share a meal. Dinnertime is a chance to refresh, refuel, and refocus. To bring that focus back to Christ during the holidays, you can make a conversation jar to steer you in the right direction.

Purchase a Christmas jar or canister, or decorate one of your own. On 2"x 4" strips of paper, write questions that pertain to Christmas. Fold the strips and place them in the jar. During dinner each night in December, have a different family member pull a question from the jar. Then go around the table, taking turns giving answers.

Below are a few questions to get you started, but part of the fun is coming up with your own.

❖ Describe the sounds that might have been heard in the stable on Christmas night.

❖ Who do you think took care of the sheep when the shepherds ran off to see baby Jesus?

❖ Describe a Christmas tree to a blind person.

❖ What do you think the wise men wore when they visited Jesus?

❖ What smells do you imagine were in the stable?

❖ What do you think the animals were thinking after Jesus was born?

❖ What is your favorite Christmas present ever?

❖ What Christmas tradition means the most to you?

❖ How much light does it take to drive out darkness?

❖ What are some amazing facts about the Christmas story?

❖ What is your favorite Christmas carol?

❖ What is your favorite Christmas smell?

❖ What is your favorite Christmas food?

❖ What is your favorite Christmas memory?

❖ Describe how the sky looked when the angels appeared to the shepherds.

❖ Which person in the Christmas story would you like to have been?

Evangelistic Opportunities

Hearts are more open to hear about the Christ-child at Christmas than at any other time of the year. The same people who normally would be offended by an open testimony about Jesus and the salvation He brings almost expect it during the holidays.

One way to seize the opportunity is to host a Christmas coffee or tea for the women in your neighborhood. They will love the opportunity to catch up with old friends and meet new acquaintances.

Joyce Bademan, in her book, *Christmas Gatherings*, offers the following suggestions. (See Appendix A for ordering the book.) The first week of December, mail or hand deliver invitations to each household in your neighborhood. On the invitation note, "A friend will share some inspiring thoughts on Christmas."

During the party, after everyone has enjoyed the holiday goodies for about forty-five minutes, the hostess gathers the group into one room and asks each person to share a favorite Christmas tradition. Then the hostess's friend, who is usually someone not from the neighborhood, shares very simply what Christmas means to her, including the true meaning of Christmas and the gospel message in a non-threatening way.

I've hosted such a gathering, and I've been the friend who shared the message at other parties. No Christmas experience can compare to having a part in seeing someone come to Christ.

Another opportunity awaits as you send out Christmas cards. Make sure to include a message about the Christ-child and why He came.

Family Devotions

*E*ven the best-intentioned families get caught up in the swirl of holiday activities only to collapse in their beds at night and rise the next day to do it all over again. The only way to keep your family devotions intact during Christmas is to have a plan.

Set aside time each night. Make Bible reading as vital and interesting as possible. It will come alive by asking questions such as, "What sounds do you suppose the shepherds heard while sitting on the hillside before the angels appeared?" "What's your favorite word in this verse?" "What is the opposite of joy? Peace?"

Have a Christmas worship center for the holidays. It could be around the nativity, by the advent wreath, or in a room lit only by the Christmas tree's twinkling lights.

A lit candle makes any occasion special; so light a candle during family devotions and remind your family that the Light of the World is the reason we celebrate Christmas.

If your family isn't in the habit of having family devotions, what a great time to start!

Gifts for Jesus

Whoever heard of going to a birthday celebration and everyone receiving a present except the birthday child? This Christmas, let's make the "guest of honor" the first person on our gift list.

But what do you give the "Man who has everything?" You give Him your heart, your obedience, your love, your anger, your bitterness. Why, He even takes your burdens and accepts them as precious gifts.

This Christmas, think of something you would like to give the Christ-child. Perhaps little Johnny would like to give Jesus his bad attitude about his sister. Perhaps Dad would like to give up that grudge he's been holding against a coworker. Maybe Mom would like to give Jesus the gift of spending more time in prayer.

Let each person decide what present to give the Christ-child and privately write the item on a piece of paper. Fold the pieces and place them in a small box. Finally, wrap the box and place it by the manger on Christmas morning.

My Gift

What can I give Him,

Poor as I am?

If I were a shepherd

I would give Him a lamb.

If I were a wise man,

I would do my part.

But what can I give Him?

I will give Him my heart.

— Christina G. Rossetti

H

Helping Others

"Then the King will say to those on His right, 'Come, you who are blessed of My Father, inherit the kingdom prepared for you from the foundation of the world. For I was hungry, and you gave Me something to eat; I was thirsty, and you gave me drink; I *was a stranger, and you invited me in; naked and you clothed Me; I was sick, and you vis-*

ited me; I was in prison, and you came to Me.' Then the righteous will answer Him, saying,

'Lord, when did we see You hungry, and feed You, or thirsty, and give You drink? And when

did we see You a stranger, and invite You in, or naked, and clothe You? And when did we see

You sick, or in prison, and come to You?' And the King will answer and say to them, 'Truly

I say to you, to the extent that you did it to one of these brothers of Mine, even the least of

them, you did it to Me'" (Matthew 25:34-40).

One of the best ways to celebrate a Christ-centered Christmas is to help others in need. When we spend time in the local soup kitchen, pack a shoebox for destitute children overseas, or deliver presents to children whose parents are incarcerated, we are ministering to Jesus Christ Himself. We also are opening our children's eyes to the needs of those around us.

Not everyone lives in a warm, secure home with three meals a day, sleeps in a cozy bed, and has a family that loves him. Breaking out of our protective cocoon and helping those who are less fortunate keeps our perspective in this materialistic, self-centered, commercialized society. Celebrating a Christ-centered Christmas is about giving of our resources, our time, and ourselves.

Here are a few ideas for your family:

❖ Help an elderly person decorate his or her home. (And take down the decorations at the end of the season!)

❖ Give an anonymous gift of money to someone who has been laid off or who you know struggles financially.

❖ Offer to Christmas shop for a disabled person.

❖ Purchase and deliver a gift for a child whose parent is in prison. (For more information on an organization that oversees this project each year, see Project Angel Tree in Appendix A.)

❖ Participate in Operation Christmas Child by packing a shoebox for a needy child overseas. (See Appendix A.)

❖ Sort toys for the Salvation Army.

❖ Volunteer to ring the bell for the Salvation Army.

❖ Work in a soup kitchen.

❖ Visit someone in a nursing home who has few relatives.

❖ Give a pint of blood.

❖ Let the children hand deliver a cash donation to your favorite charity.

❖ Baby-sit in a homeless shelter for women and children so the mothers can have a break.

Inexpensive Gift-Giving

What does inexpensive gift-giving have to do with celebrating a Christ-centered Christmas? When you consider that $2.8 million dollars were put on credit cards every ten minutes between Thanksgiving and Christmas in 1998, you realize that our focus has been more on buying gifts than on celebrating the Gift. When we are less concerned about our pocketbook's depletion, our minds are freer to focus on the Christ-child. And as Jesus so wonderfully demonstrated, the best gifts can neither be bought nor sold.

Here are a few inexpensive gift ideas that will touch the heart but leave the pocketbook intact.

❖ Make coupon booklets for your children. "This coupon is good for one game of Monopoly," "for having me stop lecturing you when you think I'm overreacting," "for a dozen donuts," "for an hour past curfew," "for a steak dinner," "for a hug," etc.

❖ Make a coupon booklet for your spouse. I'll let you come up with the suggestions!

❖ Write letters. Actions do speak louder than words, but people need words too. Write a letter to your spouse or your children telling what you appreciate about them and why you are glad they belong to you.

❖ Give something of your own that a friend or relative has admired. The mother of a college friend of mine gave me a beautiful Stratfordshire blue antique plate that I had admired. It's one of my treasured possessions.

❖ Make a scrapbook for your children, your parents, or your spouse.

❖ Copy your favorite recipes on cards and give to a newlywed.

❖ Write a letter to the person chiefly responsible for leading you to the Lord.

❖ Make a video of your children to send to relatives who live far away. (Grandma and Grandpa would much rather receive this than another pair of bedroom slippers.)

Long Walk Part of Gift

An African boy listened carefully as the teacher explained why it is that Christians give presents to each other on Christmas day. "The gift is an expression of our joy over the birth of Jesus and our friendship for each other," she said.

When Christmas day came, the boy brought to the teacher a seashell of lustrous beauty.

"Where did you ever find such a beautiful shell?" the teacher asked as she gently fingered the gift.

The youth told her that there was only one spot where such extraordinary shells could be found. When he named the place, a certain bay several miles away, the teacher was speechless.

"Why…why, it's gorgeous…wonderful, but you shouldn't have gone all that way to get a gift for me."

His eyes brightening, the boy answered, "Long walk part of gift." [2]

Jesse Tree

A popular saying in the
old South was, "Who are your
people?" In other words, old
southerners wanted to know

about their acquaintance's family tree. One look at 1 and 2 Chronicles tells us that family trees also are important to God.

A Jesse Tree is a tree decorated with symbols of Jesus' heritage. Much like the advent calendar, twenty-five decorations—one for each of the first twenty-five days of December—highlight Old Testament stories, characters, and prophesies leading up to Christ's birth and are displayed on a tree.

Begin with a small globe representing creation; then an apple with a snake showing the fall of man; followed by Noah's ark; Abraham's tent; and so on. The tree itself can be a small artificial spruce or a simple branch secured in a flowerpot with plaster of Paris. The symbols can be colored on three-inch poster board circles or constructed with felt, beads, and various craft supplies.

Ann Hibbard's book, *Family Celebrations at Christmas*, offers patterns that can be traced along with a devotional guide for each symbol.

For a more elaborate version of the Jesse Tree, Carol McCray has designed a quilted wall hanging that can be passed down from generation to generation. (Ordering information is in Appendix A.) This beautiful heirloom is shaped like a Christmas tree, and the ornaments, with brightly colored felt and other fabrics, accented with ribbons, sequins, beads, yarn, and fabric paint, are designed to appeal to children. A variety of mate-rials, including sticks, stones, paper, and fur, gives a range of textures that intrigue children. Construction techniques are simple and spelled out clearly so that anyone who can thread a needle can create this project. (I would suggest starting in the summer to give you plenty of time. Remember, it needs to be

complete by December 1.)

The kit also comes with "The Jesse Tree Journey" booklet that includes a Scripture for each ornament, discussion questions, songs, prayer suggestions, and other activities to reinforce or expand the lesson.

Your children will be so intrigued by this rendition of the Jesse Tree that they may not let you take it down after the holiday season has passed!

Kitchen Jars

As soon as the Thanksgiving dinner table is cleared, Christmas begins. Thanksgiving's newspaper is bulging—not with articles on how people gave thanks but with retail circulars boasting incredible sales and warning, "Only twenty-nine more shopping days 'til Christmas!"

It's not easy to keep our focus on the Christ-child during the holidays. Long shopping lists, a plethora of cookies to bake, parties to attend, Christmas pageants to view, a home to decorate, packages to mail, meals to prepare, and cards to address can overwhelm us.

I keep two simple jars in my kitchen to remind me where my focus needs to be. One jar is filled with fist-sized rocks. The other is three-fourths full of sand. I've discovered that I can pour all the sand into the rock jar, with the grains filling in nicely around the rocks. However, if I try to wedge the rocks into the jar three-fourths full of sand, the rocks won't fit. As the innkeeper said, "There is no room."

In my life, the large rocks represent the things that God wants me to do:

spend time with Him each day praying and reading His Word, love and support my husband, and nurture and care for my child with whom God has blessed me.

The sand represents my to-do list, which is as endless as the sand grains: decorating, baking, running erands, etc. If I begin my day with the rocks, then all the sand will fit into place. But if I start my day with the sand, somehow the rocks never seem to fit in.

Consider making two jars of your own to help keep your focus on Jesus Christ this Christmas. Tie a beautiful bow around each one and place them in a visible spot. And remember, Jesus is our rock and our redeemer (Psalm 19:14).

Love, 1 Corinthians 13-Style

If I decorate my house perfectly with plaid bows, strands of twinkling lights, and shiny glass balls but do not show love to my family, I'm just another decorator.

If I slave away in the kitchen, baking dozens of Christmas cookies, preparing gourmet meals, and arranging a beautifully adorned table at mealtime but do not show love to my family, I'm just another cook.

If I work at the soup kitchen, carol in the nursing home, and give all that I have to charity but do not show love to my family, it profits me nothing.

If I trim the spruce with shimmering angels and crocheted snowflakes, attend a myriad of holiday parties, and sing in the choir's cantata but do not focus on Christ, I have missed the point.

Love stops the cooking to hug the child.

Love sets aside the decorating to kiss the husband.

Love is kind, though harried and tired.

Love doesn't envy another's home that has coordinated Christmas china and table linens.

Love doesn't yell at the kids to get out of the way.

Love doesn't give only to those who are able to give in return but rejoices in giving to those who can't.

Love bears all things, believes all things, hopes all things, endures all things.

Love never fails. Video games will break; pearl necklaces will be lost; golf clubs will rust. But giving the gift of love will endure.

—*Sharon Jaynes*

Manger: Where Is Baby Jesus?

The prophets of old anticipated the coming of the Christ-child. Simeon and the prophetess, Anna, waited their entire lives in the Jerusalem temple to see the promise of His coming fulfilled. We too can create an atmosphere of expectancy in our homes by setting out a nativity scene but leaving the manger empty.

Each day of December, as the children walk by the empty manger, they will ask, "Where's baby Jesus?" And we can reply, "He's not here yet. But He's coming soon!"

To enhance the idea of preparing for His arrival, have the children add a few sprigs of straw to make Jesus' bed cozy. Then, on Christmas morning, before little feet make their way to the crèche, place the baby Jesus in His manger bed. The children will bound into the room with cries of, "He's here! He's here! Baby Jesus is here!"

But one word of caution: Don't forget where you put baby Jesus!

Nativity Scene

*N*ativity sets come in all shapes and sizes: crystal figurines displayed on mirrored bases; intricate wooden carvings clustered in roughly hewn stables; delicate china with hand-painted faces; and plastic, life-sized statues that illuminate front lawns. Whatever set you choose, having a nativity scene that children can play with will help cement in their minds Christmas's true meaning.

One such idea is a cloth, soft-sculpted set that will provide years of creative play. Imagine a child reenacting the Christmas story time and time again as he marches the camels across the den floor, quotes the angels' majestic announcement, and coddles baby Jesus in his arms. In Appendix B are four simple patterns that you can use to create your own soft-sculpted nativity.

Another of my favorite nativity sets comes from Bethlehem, and its pieces are crudely carved from olive trees in the Holy Land. The nine pieces fit snugly in a small pouch for storage. Because of the porous nature of the wood, after years of children's play, the oil from their hands is absorbed into the wood until it becomes dark and smooth. What a treasure to pass down to your children's children!

Open Heart, Open Home

Christmas can be the most joyful time of the year, a time surrounded by family and friends exchanging gifts and hugs. But for many, Christmas is a depressing time that echoes feelings of loneliness and isolation.

Whether separated from family by distance or alone because of estrangement or death, for these people, the holidays magnify the emptiness. Currier and Ives Christmas cards of a horse drawn sleigh making its way to a candlelit bungalow with smoke curling from the chimney, commercials of partygoers laughing happily while sipping eggnog and standing under the mistletoe, families worshipping together in church pews with Dad's arm lovingly placed around Mom while two polished children stand by their side—all of these tug at the hearts of those who are alone during the holidays.

Do you know a college student away from home, a widow or divorcee who will be eating Christmas dinner alone? Celebrate a Christ-centered Christmas by sharing your traditions with others. Invite them into your home. Encourage them to participate in the reading of the Christmas story in Luke 2. Give them a gift. Let them help with the cleanup—that will really make them feel at home! Opening your home to others may even lead them to opening their hearts to the Christ-child for the first time.

Prayer for Those Who Send You Christmas Cards

The author of Hebrews 7:25 notes that Jesus lives to intercede for those who draw near to Him. We also can be intercessors as we focus on Christ during Christmas. Let's make use of those Christmas cards that pile up in our homes. Place the cards in a basket by the kitchen table. Each night, as the family gathers for dinner, have a member select and read a card. Then join hands and pray for the fam-

ily or individual who sent the greeting. This can also be done at breakfast or during family devotions.

Praying for the senders of Christmas cards doesn't have to stop after the holidays, but could be carried over into the new year until each person has been lifted up to God's throne. If other people hear about your family's tradition, be prepared for a flood of cards from individuals you barely know!

Quick and Easy Crafts for Kids

*I*nevitably some days Mom and Dad will be busy with Christmas preparations. So keep the children's little fingers occupied. Below are some craft ideas that focus on the Christmas story:

Beaded Cross

Materials:

- Two metallic gold pipe cleaners (chenille stems)
- A bag of 6mm, clear plastic crystal beads

Instructions:

Cut one pipe cleaner in half. Twist it around the other pipe cleaner, forming a simple cross. Thread the beads onto the four arms of the cross until it is full. Bend the two sides and bottom arms to secure the beads in place. Place a loop of gold thread at the top of the long pipe cleaner and fold the top of the pipe cleaner down, securing the loop in place. Add a drop of hot glue or craft glue to secure the ends. Hang it on the tree or give to a friend as a gift.

Pomander Balls

Materials:

- 1 medium orange
- Round toothpicks
- 1 bottle of whole cloves
- Powdered cinnamon or nutmeg (spices might be less expensive if

purchased at a craft store)

Instructions:

With a round toothpick, poke shallow holes into the peel of an orange. Poke the pointed end of a clove into the hole. Put as many cloves as you like, but leave some space (about the size of one clove) between each clove to allow for shrinkage when the orange dries. When the clove-studded orange is full, roll it in a mixture of ground nutmeg and cinnamon. Place the pomanders in a decorative bowl or hang them from the tree by a ribbon attached to the top of each orange with hot glue. The spices will fill the room with the wonderful scents of Christmas. Explain to the children that one of the gifts the magi brought to the Christ-child was frankincense, which was also an aromatic spice.

Angel Banner

Materials:

- Large white men's handkerchief or white cloth napkin
- Tempura paint
- One precious child
- One 1/2-inch diameter wooden dowel rod
- Ribbon or braid

Instructions:

Mix the paint to create a thin consistency. Pour a small amount into a paper plate. Dip the bottom of the child's foot in the paint. Blot the foot to remove any excess. Stamp the cloth with the foot, making a footprint. The heel will be the angel's head.

Now dip the right hand in the paint. Blot to remove excess. Use the hand to create the angel's right wing, placing the palm next to the curve (arch) of the footprint with the fingers pointing out.

Repeat, using the left hand to create the left wing. Let the paint dry thoroughly. Cut the dowel so that it is one to two inches longer than the width of the cloth. You may want to spray paint it metallic gold.

Wrap the edge of the cloth around the dowel rod and secure it in place. You can sew a rod pocket and slip the dowel through, or secure the banner in place with hot glue or Velcro.

Tie the ends of a piece of pretty ribbon or braid to each end of the dowel. Now the banner is ready to hang!

Baker's Dough Ornaments

Materials:

- 1/3 cup of water
- 1/2 cup of salt
- 1 cup of all-purpose flour

• Paint and paintbrushes

• Varnish

• Ribbon or yarn

Instructions:

Mix the salt, water, and flour in a bowl. Knead with your hands to form a smooth consistency. Roll out the dough (with a rolling pin) on a smooth surface. Use cookie cutters that tell the Christmas story (angel, tree, star, bell, etc.) to cut out various shapes. Place each shape on a baking sheet covered with aluminum foil. Make a hole in the top of each shape with a straw. Bake at 275 degrees for one hour or until brown. They should be hard, but not burned.

Paint the shapes when they are cooled completely. (I use acrylic paints.) When the paint is dry, spray or brush on a coat of varnish. Let dry.

Thread a ribbon or piece of yarn through the hole and hang the ornament on your tree. You may want to write your child's name and date on the back.

"Ready" Redefined

$\mathcal{E}$ verywhere you go during December people ask the same question. At the grocery checkout counter you hear, "Are you ready for Christmas?"

At the bank drive-through window you're asked, "Are you ready for Christmas?" Even at the doctor's office the question comes, "Are you ready for Christmas?"

Actually, I think the answer to that question depends on how you define "ready." Reflect for a moment on the words of this poem and then answer the question, "Are you ready for Christmas?"

"Ready for Christmas," she said with a sigh

As she gave a last touch to the gifts piled high...

Then wearily sat for a moment and read

Till soon, very soon, she was nodding her head.

Then quietly spoke a voice in her dream,

"Ready for Christmas, what do you mean?"

She woke with a start and a cry of despair.

"There's so little time, and I've still to prepare.

Oh, Father, forgive me, I see what You mean!

Yes, more than the giving of gifts and a tree,

It's the heart swept clean that He wanted to see,

A heart that is free from bitterness and sin.

So be ready for Christmas—and ready for Him".

———Author Unknown [3]

Singing the Gospel

When my son was four years old, I overheard him singing "O Holy Night" in his best vibrato. I chuckled as he belted out, "Long lay the world in sin and ever whining." While "error pining" wasn't in his vocabulary, he definitely understood the concept of whining.

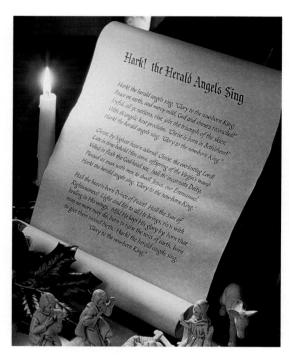

The words to Christmas carols explain the gospel in a rich and wonderful way. I can still remember several years ago the exhilaration I felt when I heard "Joy to the world, the Lord has come" played over a department store's intercom. A preacher on a soapbox would have been offensive, but the sweet music on the intercom sang the gospel while shoppers hummed along.

During the holiday season, take advantage of the richness of carols to teach about the Christ-child to your family or as a message at a Christmas tea, as mentioned in "E – Evangelistic Opportunities" in this book.

For example, let's look at "Hark! the Herald Angels Sing."

Have someone read the first verse and then ask, "Did you ever wonder why the angels were so excited?" The next line gives us a hint: "Glory to the newborn King."

The following line reads, "Peace on earth and mercy mild, God and sinners reconciled!" Some people aren't too crazy about the word "sinner." But originally it referred to archery. "Sin" was the distance between the bull's eye and where the arrow landed on the target. Therefore, "sin" meant "to miss the mark." And it still means that today; sin refers to missing the mark of God's perfection. The Bible states that all have sinned and fallen short of God's perfect character. Because of that sin, we're separated from God.

The first verse of "Hark! the Herald Angels Sing" tells us *why* Jesus came: to reconcile or join us back together with God. It also tells us to whom Jesus came: "to all nations." Look at all the exclamation marks. No wonder the angels were so excited!

Have someone read verse two. If verse one tells us why Jesus came, verse two tells us *who* He was.

Can you list all the descriptions of Jesus found in verse two? He is adored in heaven. He is the everlasting Lord. He is the offspring of a virgin's womb. He is God with flesh and bones. He is deity. He is Emmanuel, which means, "God with us."

Have someone read verse three. This verse tells us *how* the Christ-child made eternal life available to all humans. He laid aside His glorious heavenly position, came to earth as a man, and gave His life so that we could experience a second birth and live eternally in heaven.

Packed into this one Christmas carol we learn *why* Jesus came, *who* He was, and *how* He would reconcile us with the Father. Now pick out another carol and see what treasures are tucked inside.

'Twas the Night Before Jesus Came

'Twas the night before Christmas and all through the house, not a creature was stirring, not even a mouse. Wait a minute, what does this familiar story have to do with celebrating a Christ-centered Christmas?

I suggest reading a new rendition to your older children. You might even want to leave *Celebrating a Christ-Centered Christmas* open to this page on your coffee table.

Twas the night before Jesus came

And all through the house,

Not a creature was praying,

Not one in the house.

Their Bibles were lying on the shelf without care,

In hopes that Jesus would not come there.

The children were dressing to crawl into bed,

Not once ever kneeling or bowing a head.

And Mom in her rocker with baby on her lap,

Was watching the late show, while I took a nap.

When out of the east there arose such a clatter,

I sprang to my feet to see what was the matter.

Away to the window, I flew like a flash.

I tore back the shutters and threw back the sash.

And what to my wondering eyes should appear,

But angels proclaiming that Jesus was here.

With a light like the sun, sending forth a bright ray,

I knew in a moment, this must be the day.

The light of His face made me cover my head.

It was Jesus returning, just like He said.

And though I possessed worldly wisdom and wealth,

I cried when I saw Him, in spite of myself.

In the Book of Life, which He held in His hand,

Was written the name of every saved man.

He spoke not a word as

He searched for my name.

And when He said, "It's not here,"

I hung my head in shame.

The people whose names had been written with love,

He gathered to take to His Father above.

With all those who were ready, He rose without a sound,

While all the rest were left standing around.

I fell to my knees, but it was too late.

I'd waited too long, thus sealed my fate.

I stood and I cried as they rode out of sight.

If only I'd been ready tonight.

In the words of this poem, the meaning is clear,

The coming of Jesus is drawing near.

There's only one life and when comes the last call,

We'll find that the Bible was right after all.

—Author Unknown[4]

Unforgettable

*H*ave you ever flipped through a photo album and gazed at a picture of a moment in your child's life, and then thought, *Now, let's see, was Steven in the second or third grade when that picture was taken? And who is that little boy that he looks so chummy with?*

Ten, twenty, or thirty years can rob you of the treasures stored in your memory bank. Precious happenings that you thought you always would remember become fuzzier with the passing years.

Since we're going to celebrate a Christ-centered Christmas this year, let's make sure those memories truly are unforgettable. Each Christmas, take a picture of everyone who celebrated the day

with your family. Place one or two photos in a Christmas memory book. Beautiful

memory books are available at retail outlets, or you can make one yourself. Write the

year at the top of the page and then include the names of any guests in the

pictures, special gifts that were given, and how you celebrated the day.

Also include a chronicle of the past year, listing special events, awards, new

friends, trials the family endured, and special interests of each family mem-

ber. Weave in the spiritual aspects of how the family grew in its relation-

ship with the Lord that year and any milestones that were reached.

If your children are older, don't feel it's too late to start this family tra-

dition. Even if your children are married, think of all the wonderful years ahead of you

that can be savored.

The Christmas memory book will become a storehouse of treasures that can be

handed down from generation to generation. As those who come after you read about

your family's history and faith in God, you will be passing the baton of faith to your

children and your children's children.

Variety of Simple Gestures

"And suddenly there was with the angel a multitude of the heavenly host praising God, and saying, 'Glory to God in the highest, and on earth peace, good will toward men'" (Luke 2:13 KJV).

Christmas traditionally has been a time of spreading "good will" toward men, but many can't really tell you why. Speculations include: "Because Kris Kringle dropped gold coins down stockings hanging out to dry that belonged to three poor girls who had no money for a dowry." "Because Santa brings toys to all the good little girls and boys around the world on Christmas Eve." "Because it's the Christmas spirit."

The truth is Christmas is a time to spread good will because, on that starry night in Bethlehem, as the ultimate act of kindness, God sent His Son in the form of a babe—a Son who was a gift to humankind, a redeemer, a Savior.

Now, during the holiday season, we can use a variety of simple gestures to show good will to those around us in honor of the Christ-child. Here are a few suggestions:

❖ Offer your extra tree clippings to someone who has an artificial tree to add the wonderful scent of pine to their home.

❖ Have a Silent Night in your house. Turn off the TV and radio.

❖ Send a Christmas card to someone in a nursing home who has no family.

❖ Cook a meal for a weary friend.

❖ Walk a neighbor's dog.

❖ Baby-sit for a young couple whose date night funds are tight.

❖ Shovel snow from a neighbor's sidewalk.

❖ During heavy traffic, let a car slip into the lane in front of you.

❖ Give to the Salvation Army kettle.

❖ Put a "Jesus is the Reason for the Season" sticker on checks, restaurant tabs, your child's lunch bag, anything.

❖ Tip the grocery bagger and say, "Merry Christmas."

❖ Put your shopping buggy back in its place.

❖ Write "Happy Birthday, Jesus" on your checks.

❖ Say "thank you."

❖ Let a mother with small children in front of you in the grocery line.

❖ Pay a toll for someone behind you on the highway.

❖ Fly a birthday flag on Christmas Day.

❖ Give out candy canes.

❖ Sneak a note in a friend's stocking, to be found on Christmas morning.

❖ Deliver Christmas cookies to the fire department.

❖ Phone a faraway relative on Christmas morning.

❖ Play Christmas music often.

❖ Let someone have the parking spot you found.

❖ Put a reminder of Jesus in every room of your house.

❖ Make sweet rolls for neighbors that can be baked on Christmas morning.

Sweet Roll Recipe

3/4 cup warm water

3/4 cup warm milk

2 tablespoons yeast

1 1/2 teaspoons salt

3/4 cup sugar

3/4 cup margarine

2 eggs

6 3/4 cups bread flour

Mix all the ingredients together and allow the dough to rise until doubled. (About 1-2 hours.) Divide the dough in half. Roll out in a rectangle. Sprinkle cinnamon crumbs over the dough.

Cinnamon crumbs:

1 cup sugar

1 tablespoon cinnamon

1 stick margarine, melted

Roll the dough into a jellyroll shape. Slice into circular rolls 3/8" thick. Place on a greased pan. Bake at 350 degrees for 20 minutes, covered with foil. Remove foil and cook for 10 minutes more. Let cool. Frost with confectioner's sugar icing.

Sugar Icing:

1 1/2 cup 10X confectioner's sugar

2 tablespoons margarine, melted

2 tablespoons milk

Stir ingredients together and pour over the rolls.

Makes two 9" x 12" pans of rolls.

Make these ahead of time and store them in the freezer. Remove them on Christmas Eve and let them thaw. Pop them in the oven on Christmas Day. They are great to share with neighbors and friends.

Wise Men: Who Are Those Guys Anyway?

*Q*uite a bit of confusion has existed over the years about the "Wee Three Kings of Orientar," as some, in their puzzlement, call these three guys. Were they wise men?

Magi? Kings? How old was Jesus when they arrived? Did they visit Jesus on Christmas night? Or was Jesus a toddler by the time they arrived? What's with those strange gifts? The rough and rowdy Herdmans in *The Greatest Christmas Pageant Ever* thought a ham was a much more practical gift than gold, frankincense, and myrrh.

Matthew 2:1-12 tells the story of the "wise men" (as they are called in

the King James Version) or "magi" (in the New American Standard Version) who came from the east to worship the new king of the Jews. Traditionally these travelers have been referred to as kings, but Scripture doesn't confirm that. We don't know exactly how many of them there were, but again, traditionally we've believed there were three because of the three gifts.

Most likely these wise guys didn't show up in the stable at Christ's birth. Matthew 2:11 says that they "came into the house and saw the

Child," indicating that Mary and Joseph had moved from the stable. We're not sure how old Jesus was when they arrived. Some sources say He might have been two years old.

Apparently, God didn't think these details were important. But He did give specific information about the gifts the wise men brought for Jesus: gold, frankincense, and myrrh. Gold stood for the riches of a king; Jesus was the King of Kings. Frankincense was a type of incense used by the priests in the temple worship; Jesus would be our high priest who would intercede for us to the heavenly Father. And myrrh was a perfume used in burial services, pointing to Jesus' death on the cross—a holy sacrifice for our sins.

One way for you to emphasize the wise men's journey is to place the figures a short distance away from the nativity displayed in your home. Each day, move the trio a little closer, until they finally arrive on Christmas Day.

"X" Marks the Spot

*E*veryone loves a treasure hunt, and it makes a wonderful Christmas activity. Write a series of clues on individual pieces of paper. Tell the children the starting point, such as on the front door. On the front door, post a clue that will lead them to the second clue. When they discover that second clue, have the third clue posted, and so on. Here are some suggestions for clues that anyone can use:

- ❖ This always appears twice as dirty as it is. *(mirror)*
- ❖ This is Mom's least favorite appliance in the house. *(In my house that would be the iron!)*
- ❖ This clue has some chilling features. *(in the refrigerator)*
- ❖ This clue will make your heart sing. *(CD or tape player)*
- ❖ Now you're on a roll. *(paper towel dispenser)*
- ❖ Don't expect to be spoon-fed. *(silverware drawer)*
- ❖ The final clue: Where your treasure is, there your heart will be also. *(Have the location for the treasure written on a piece of paper tucked inside the family Bible.)*

After the treasure hunt, as you celebrate with cups of hot cocoa, explain that locating the Christ-child for people who lived during his time was also much like a treasure hunt. God had given the people many clues to help them know where He would be born, who His ancestors would be, and what He would do once He came.

Then read the following verses and ask the children to point out what clues they can find in each.

❖ *Isaiah 7:14*

❖ *Isaiah 9:2-7*

❖ *Isaiah 11:1-3*

❖ *Isaiah 40:11*

❖ *Isaiah 60:1,2*

❖ *Micah 5:2*

Yearly Traditions

While advertisers boast slogans of "new and improved" to the consumer, it's comforting to know that some things never change. Yearly traditions bring continuity to a constantly changing world. Family traditions are the lighthouse beacon that welcomes ships passing in the night, inviting them to drop anchor in a safe harbor.

Surround your family with familiar sights, sounds, and tastes at Christmas. Let the echoes of past generations hug your spirits and refresh, refuel, and reassure your souls. Below are some ideas for yearly traditions that can give a sense of stability and cohesiveness. This year, pick one or two to incorporate into your holiday season.

❖ Watch "It's a Wonderful Life."

❖ Open one present each on Christmas Eve. Let it be a new pair of flannel pajamas to be donned on Christmas morn.

❖ Take a family photo in front of the tree each year.

❖ Scatter a puzzle on a table in the family room the weekend after Thanksgiving. Work on it sporadically and try to have it finished by

Christmas Day.

❖ Take your family to hear a performance of Handel's "Messiah."

❖ Read Luke 2 by candlelight before going to bed on Christmas Eve.

❖ Make placing the angel on the top of the tree the crescendo of the tree-decorating festivities.

❖ Decorate the tree while listening to the same Christ-centered Christmas music every year.

❖ Read Christmas bedtime stories during December. (*The Greatest Christmas Pageant Ever* is my favorite.)

❖ Decorate the tree on the same day each year. Our family decorates on the Sunday following Thanksgiving.

❖ Volunteer to work at the same charity each year.

❖ Wait until Christmas morning to place baby Jesus in the manger.

❖ Watch Scrooge in "A Christmas Carol" on video.

❖ Listen to Focus on the Family's audio version of "A Christmas Carol."

❖ Record a cheerful, Christ-centered greeting on your answering machine.

❖ Attend a Christmas Eve candlelight service with your family.

❖ Start a collection (stamp, coin, etc.) for your child. Add to that collection each year.

❖ Give each child a Christmas ornament each year that reflects his or her interests. When that child marries, give him or her the collection as a wedding gift. (Buy yourself an extra box of tissues for when you hand the ornaments over.)

❖ Videotape family members opening presents every year.

❖ Serve the same breakfast menu every Christmas morning.

❖ Fill a basket with old Christmas photos and set them on your coffee table.

❖ Line your sidewalk or driveway with luminaries on Christmas Eve. Use white lunch bags filled with two inches of sand and a votive candle set in the center.

❖ Decorate a second tree with all the children's and grandchildren's homemade ornaments.

❖ Wrap your child's bedroom door with pretty gift paper to

transform it into a giant package.

❖ Record the family singing Christmas carols on a cassette tape. (Send a copy to grandparents who live far away or save it for the family archives.)

❖ Light a large red Christmas candle each night at dinner during December.

❖ Make special cookies that you only prepare at Christmas.

❖ Drive through a highly decorated area of town and look at the lights one night.

❖ Collect Christmas ornaments that remind you of past vacations. Remember the travels as you decorate the tree.

❖ Have one special ornament that is hung first each year.

❖ Lace green and red shoe strings in your family's tennis shoes.

❖ Give a family member a gag gift. The following year, have that person wrap the same gift and give it to another family member. Do this year after year. It will be fun to see who gets the prize each year.

The Jayneses Family Christmas Breakfast

Breakfast Before

So called because it's made the night before and simply cooked on Christmas day.

- 1 pound of pork sausage
- 6 eggs
- 2 cups milk
- 2 slices bread, cubed
- 1 cup of sharp cheddar cheese, grated
- 1 teaspoon salt
- 1 teaspoon dry mustard

Sauté the sausage, drain all the grease, and set aside. Beat the eggs. Combine milk, salt, and mustard, and stir into the eggs. Layer the bread cubes on the bottom of a 9" x 13" baking dish. Then layer the sausage, followed by the cheese. Pour the egg mixture over the top. Cover and refrigerate overnight. The next day, bake at 350 degrees for 45 minutes. Serves 6-8.

Baked Cheese Grits

2 1/2 cups milk

3/4 cup uncooked regular grits

1/2 cup margarine

1/2 teaspoon salt

1/3 cup grated parmesan cheese

1 5-oz. jar sharp process cheese spread

Bring milk to a boil. Add grits, reduce heat and cook until thickened (about 10 minutes). Stir often. Stir in margarine, salt, and both cheeses until blended. Spoon into a lightly greased 1-quart casserole dish. Bake at 325 degrees for 20 minutes. Serves 6-8.

Zion, He's Coming Again

We began our journey focusing on the "advent" or coming of Jesus Christ. Now we end by looking forward to our King's second advent. Jesus came two thousand years ago as a babe in the manger, but He has promised He will come again to reign forever in Zion. When that day occurs, we will have eternal "peace on earth."

As you read the Christmas story around the fireplace, incorporate these verses.

"In the last days, the mountain of the house of the Lord will be established as the chief of the mountains, and will be raised above the hills; and all the nations will stream to it. And many peoples will come and say, 'Come, let us go up to the mountain of the Lord, to the house of the God of Jacob; that He may teach us concerning His ways, and that we may walk in His paths, for the law will go forth from Zion, and the word of the Lord from Jerusalem.' And He will judge between the nations, and will render decisions for many peoples; and they will hammer their swords into plowshares, and their spears into pruning hooks. Nation will not lift up sword against nation, and never again will they learn war" (Isaiah 2:2-4).

"Blow a trumpet in Zion, and sound an alarm on My holy mountain! Let all the inhabitants of the land tremble, for the day of the LORD is coming; surely it is near" (Joel 2:1).

"I saw a new heaven and a new earth; for the first heaven and the first earth passed away, and there was no longer any sea. And I saw the holy city, the new Jerusalem, coming down out of heaven from God, made ready as a bride adorned for her husband. And I heard a loud voice from the throne, saying, 'Behold, the tabernacle of God is among men, and He shall dwell among them, and they shall be His peoples, and God Himself shall be among them, and He shall wipe away every tear from their eyes; and there shall no longer be any death; there shall no longer be any mourning, or crying, or pain: the first things have passed away.' And He who sits on the throne said, 'Behold, I am making all things new.' And He said, 'Write, for these words are faithful and true'" (Revelation 21:1-5).

I Had a Dream

"I had a dream, Joseph. And I don't understand it, not really. But I think it was about a birthday celebration for our Son. Well, I think that's what it was about. People had been preparing for about six weeks. Everyone had decorated their houses and bought new clothes and gone shopping many times, buying elaborate gifts. It was peculiar, though, because, you see, the gifts weren't for our Son. They wrapped them in beautiful paper, tied them with lovely bows, and stacked them under trees. Yes, trees, Joseph, right in their houses. Each household decorated a tree.

"The branches were full of glowing balls and sparkling ornaments. And a figure was on top of the tree that looked something like an angel. Oh, it was so beautiful. Everyone was laughing and happy and excited about the gifts. They gave gifts to each other, Joseph, not to our Son.

"I don't think they even knew Him. They never mentioned His name. Doesn't it seem odd for people to go to all that trouble to celebrate somebody's birthday when they don't even know Him? I had the strangest feeling that if our Son had gone to this celebration, He would have been intruding.

"Everything was beautiful, Joseph. Everyone was full of cheer. But it made me want to cry. How sad for Jesus, not to be wanted at His own birthday celebration. I'm glad that it was only a dream. What if it had been true?"

—Author Unknown

111

Appendix A

Resources

Christmas Gatherings: How to Host Evangelistic Christmas Gatherings, by Joyce Bademan.
Address: Christmas Gatherings
24904 Logan Avenue
Lakeville, MN 55044
(612) 469-4793

Project Angel Tree
c/o Prison Fellowship
Charles W. Colson
1856 Old Reston Avenue
P.O. Box 97103
Washington, D.C. 20909-7103
www.angeltree.org
(800) 398-HOPE

Operation Christmas Child
Samaritan's Purse
P.O. Box 3000

Boone, NC 28607
(828) 262-1980

Jesse Tree Wall Hanging
The Proverbs 31 Ministry, Inc.
P.O. Box 17155
Charlotte, NC 28227
(704) 849-2270

Olive Wood Nativity
The Proverbs 31 Ministry, Inc.
P.O. Box 17155
Charlotte, NC 28227
(704) 849-2270

Appendix B
Soft-Sculpted Nativity Instructions

Instructions for Soft-Sculpted Nativity Set

Materials

Fabrics:

- Subdued colors for Joseph, Mary, the Babe, and the shepherds
- Bright colors for the wise men
- White for the angel
- Felt for faces and hands

- Matching thread for each fabric
- 2-pound bag of poly-pellets
- Black acrylic paint for the eyes
- Fiberfill batting
- Sandwich bags
- Gold thread for Jesus' halo
- Doll hair: brown, black, and gray

Instructions

• Trace several copies of the pattern pieces onto white paper and cut them out. Use the adult pattern pieces for the angel, Mary, Joseph, the shepherds, and the wise men.

• Fold arm fabric in thirds and pin into position on the right side of the fabric, with raw edges hidden. Stitch to the right sides of the front. See pattern for placement.

• Pin the front and back body pieces right side together. Stitch the sides together, leaving an opening at the head and the base.

• Pin the base to the bottom opening of the body, right sides together. Ease extra fabric to fit. Stitch the base to the sides.

• Turn the body right side out.

• Put 2 cups of poly-pellets into a plastic sandwich bag, press out excess air, zip closed and place in the doll's base.

• Fill the doll firmly with fiberfill batting.

• Whip stitch the top of head closed.

• Blanket stitch or glue the felt face and hands in place. Tuck hands under sleeve.

• Use the tip of a craft paintbrush to make eyes with dots of paint.

• Glue doll hair on the heads. Use the hair to make beards as well.

• Cut a square of fabric for each character's headpiece. Secure in place with hot glue.

For Jesus

- Cut out the doll's front and back and two pieces for the blanket.
- Stitch the blanket to the sides of the front, making the blanket pieces criss-cross as shown on the pattern. Tuck the felt face under the edge of the blanket (turn down rough edges of the blanket) and glue in place. Sew front and back pieces right sides together, leaving enough room to pour in poly-pellets. Turn right side out. Fill with pellets and close the opening with a whipstitch. Place Jesus in a cozy bed lined with straw or extra cloth.

The rest is up to your imagination! You could cut a fabric circle to make a crown for the wise men, glue jewels on the wise men's clothing, tuck a stick under the shepherd's arm, glue wings on the angel's back, make a halo from a chenille stem, tie rope around the shepherds' and Joseph's waists for belts, or place Jesus in a tiny basket.

If your children are young, don't embellish with objects that could be removed and ingested. If your crew is old enough not to remove pieces, you may embellish to your heart's content.

Soft-Sculpted Nativity Patterns

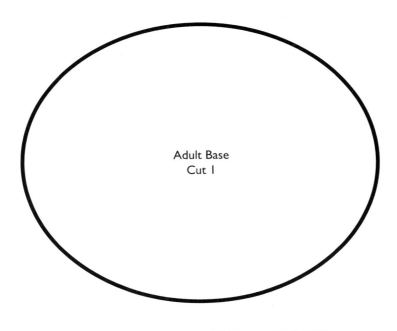

Adult Base
Cut 1

Adult Sleeve
Cut 2

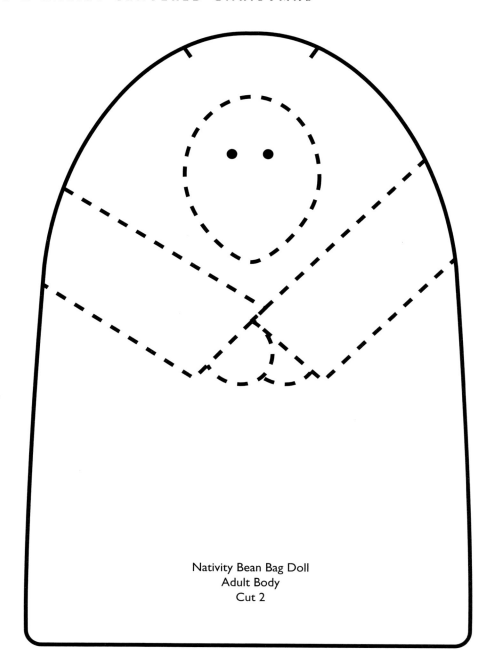

Nativity Bean Bag Doll
Adult Body
Cut 2

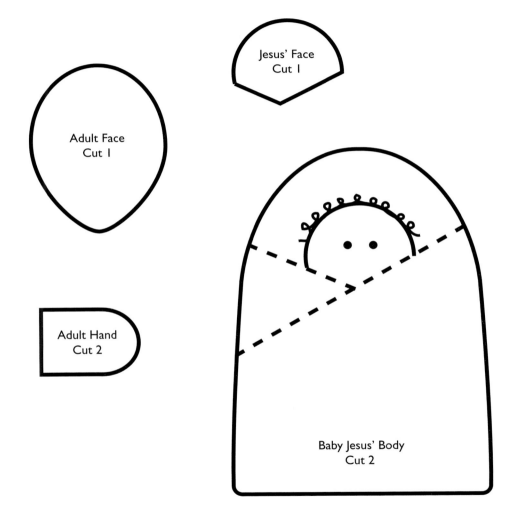

Jesus' Face
Cut 1

Adult Face
Cut 1

Adult Hand
Cut 2

Baby Jesus' Body
Cut 2

Moody Press, a ministry of Moody Bible Institute, is designed for education, evangelization, and edification.

If we may assist you in knowing more about Christ and the Christian life, please write us without obligation:

Moody Press, c/o MLM, Chicago, IL 60610.

Sharon Jaynes is the president of The Proverbs 31 Ministry, Inc., and co-host of the ministry's daily radio program.

She is also the author of *Being a Great Mom, Raising Great Kids, At Home With God: Stories of Life, Love, and Laughter* and co-author of *Seven Life Principles for Every Woman.*

Sharon is a popular speaker for women's groups all across the country and can be reached at (877) 731-4663.

For more information on the many facets of The Proverbs 31 Ministry, visit **www.proverbs31.org** or write:

The Proverbs 31 Ministry
P.O. Box 17155
Charlotte, NC 28227